LIFESKILLS

HANDBOOKS

21st CENTURY

Consumer *Spending*

Nan Bostick

and

Susan M. Freese

SADDLEBACK
EDUCATIONAL PUBLISHING

SADDLEBACK
EDUCATIONAL PUBLISHING
www.sdlback.com

ISBN-13: 978-1-61651-690-1
ISBN-10: 1-61651-690-9
eBook: 978-1-61247-342-0

Printed in Guangzhou, China
1111/CA21101811

16 15 14 13 12   1 2 3 4 5

Contents

SECTION **1**

The Wise Buyer

All shoppers love a good deal! They're thrilled when they get a top-quality item for a low price. But how do they know the quality of what they buy? And how do they know whether they're really getting a low price? Learning some principles of smart shopping will help you answer questions like these. And learning about advertising, estimates, and bargain hunting will help you avoid getting taken advantage of.

The Smartest Shopper

Lynne often met her friends at the mall on Saturdays. They loved to shop! And they especially loved to buy new clothes for going out Saturday nights.

Lynne's friend Kacie always told the group about the latest styles. She looked at lots of fashion magazines and watched fashion  shows on TV. But she didn't know much about the quality of clothes. And she never shopped around or waited for something to go on sale. She bought what she wanted, when she wanted to. She always paid full price, too!

Another friend, Grace, claimed to be a bargain hunter. She knew about all the stores that sold clothes for reduced prices. She also bought used clothes at a local shop from time to time. But Grace had

made some bad choices. She didn't always get good quality in the clothes she bought. One time, she bought some jeans for a really low price. But the first time she wore them, the zipper broke. Another time, she bought a coat that didn't really fit just because it was on sale.

Lynne was the smartest shopper. She looked around at several stores before she bought anything. She checked prices and watched for sales. She knew how to spot good quality, too. She didn't buy everything she wanted. But what she bought was well made and looked good on her. When Lynne bought a new outfit, she knew that she'd like it and wear it for longer than a weekend.

CHAPTER **1**

Principles of Smart Shopping

How to Shop

Are you a smart shopper? If not, you should learn how to make wise buying decisions. Follow these simple steps:

1. **Learn about a product before you buy it.** Read the product's label to find out what's inside the package. Also ask people who own the same product or something similar for their opinions. Do they recommend the product? Do they have any complaints about it? Ask where they purchased the product and if they got a good buy.

   Newspaper, magazine, and online ads or professional reviews can also give you facts about different *brands.* Compare the prices of different products using ads. Read articles and customer reviews to learn more about how products perform. *Consumers'* or buyers' reports are also helpful. These reports often test and grade products, showing which ones you can trust to last.

Brands

Product names or manufacturers. One product, such as a hairdryer, can be available in many brands.

Consumers

Shoppers or buyers. People who purchase goods or services for their own use.

2. **Compare what you learn about different brands.** List the advantages and disadvantages of each brand. This will help you compare different products. For instance, Tom is looking for a lightweight, waterproof watch. He's a lifeguard and needs a watch he can count on. He's made a list to help him compare features of different watches.

3. **Consider your wants and your needs.** Your wants and needs are as important as the price you pay for something. Tom's decided to buy a watch that has fewer features and costs more than the others because it's waterproof. Being waterproofs is a key feature for his work.

Where to Shop

Where you shop can make a big difference in how much you pay. Discount stores and buyer warehouses usually offer the lowest prices. But be sure you know what you want and how much its costs before you shop at one of these stores. They may sell a mix of high- and low-quality brands. You won't be able to get much customer service or advice. And you often can't try on clothes at these stores.

> ### Retail
> A kind of store that sells products one at a time for individuals' use.

Retail and specialty stores charge the highest prices. But they usually sell top-quality brands and offer good service. If you shop at a retail store, ask about upcoming sales. You can save a lot by waiting for sales, when prices are lower.

When to Shop

When you go shopping is important, too. Don't rush out to buy a new type of product the minute it's introduced. Wait for several months, when the price has probably gone down. It often pays to wait!

Prices changes on seasonal items, too. For instance, you'll pay less for a swimsuit at the end of summer than at the beginning. And you'll save money on a space heater if you buy it in the summer, not the winter.

Smart shoppers also wait for sales that occur after holidays, such as Christmas and the Fourth of July. You can often learn about these sales through newspaper or TV ads or mailers.

[FACT]

Top US Retail Chains

The following stores are listed in order of their yearly sales, from highest to lowest:

Walmart	Walgreens	Safeway
Kroger Company	CVS Caremark	SuperValu
Costco	Best Buy	Rite Aid
Home Depot	Lowe's	Publix
Target	Sears	Amazon.com

When Can You Get the Best Deals?

Products that are used at certain times of the year cost less in the off-season. Others go on sale during particular months. Plan to buy these products during these months:

January
Bedding
CDs and DVDs
Computers
TVs

February
Indoor furniture
Winter clothing

March
Winter coats
Winter sports gear

April
Computers
Spring clothing

May
Athletic clothing and
   shoes
Camping gear

June
Computers
Indoor furniture
Summer sports gear
Swimwear

July
Furniture
Swimwear

August
Air conditioners
Backpacks
Outdoor furniture

September
Bikes

October
Bikes
Computers
Winter coats

November
Bikes
TVs

December
Bikes
TVs

Interpreting Ad Copy

How Do Ads Work?

Advertisements, or ads, try to convince you to buy things or do things. First, ad writers try to get your attention:

Then, they try to convince you that you're getting a deal:

Facts versus Opinions

If an ad says "All items now on sale for half price," that's a fact. If you went into the store, you could prove that to be true or false. *Facts* are things that can be proven.

"Unbelievably low prices" isn't a fact. It's an opinion. *Opinions* are ideas or beliefs. Some people may agree with them, but others may not.

Ways to Advertise

- **Online:** Ads placed on Web sites plus social media sites
- **Direct mail:** Letters and post cards that are sent in the mail
- **Print:** Newspapers and magazines
- **Signs:** Billboards and signs on buses, and taxis
- **Television and movies:** Commercials and products used in shows
- **Radio:** Commercials and products mentioned in programs
- **Word of mouth:** People talking about the product

Can you tell the difference between facts and opinions? Read the six ads below. Which are facts and which are opinions?

1. Deal of a Lifetime!
2. All Items on Sale Till May 31
3. Nothing Over $50.00
4. Shoes Priced for Every Budget
5. Best Prices Anywhere!
6. 60-Quart Ice Chest—Only $26.99

Answers:
1. Opinion.
2. Fact.
3. Fact.
4. Opinion.
5. Opinion.
6. Fact.

Why is it important to **interpret** ads correctly? Knowing how to read ads can help you compare prices and locate the best buys. You can use ads to find a service you might need or learn about special sales or new products.

Ignore the opinions! Look only for the facts.

Interpret
To find the meaning of

Misleading
Meant to confuse or give the wrong idea

How Do Ads Convince You?

Advertisements use many different methods to try to convince you. Here are some of the most common:

→ **Misleading words:** Ad writers use words such as *new, fresh, natural, improved,* and *healthy* to make their products sound good. But don't be fooled. Look for facts to help you decide if the words are being used truthfully.

For example, *Forever Fresh* would be a good name for a brand of butter. People like to think that the food they buy is fresh. But butter won't stay fresh forever. Smart shoppers look at a product's *expiration date.* It tells when the product is no longer considered fresh or safe to eat.

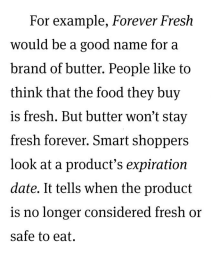

→ **Comparatives:** Nearly all ads use *comparatives,* which are words that compare things. Comparatives usually end in *-er,* such as *brighter, faster, smoother.* When you hear a comparative being used, always ask a question like "Brighter than what?" "Faster than what?" "Smoother than what?" If the ad doesn't say, then it's simply stating someone's opinion.

[FACT]

Truth in Advertising

The US government has laws that protect consumers from false or misleading ads. Advertisers must have proof that their claims are true and fair. If you become a victim of false advertising, you have the right to file a complaint. The Federal Trade Commission (FTC) enforces advertising laws. To file a complaint, go online to the FTC's Web site (www.ftccomplaintassistant.gov).

→ **Exaggerations:** Ad writers tend to *exaggerate.* They often say things are bigger, better, cheaper, or more important than they really are. Exaggerations get your attention and make you want to act right away.

Exaggerate

To claim that something is more than it really is.

Here's an example of an exaggeration:

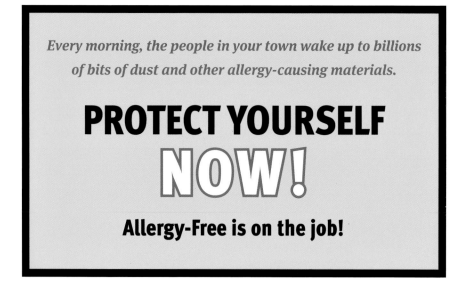

Every morning, the people in your town wake up to billions of bits of dust and other allergy-causing materials.

PROTECT YOURSELF
NOW!

Allergy-Free is on the job!

Ask questions if you think an ad exaggerates. Are there really billions of bits of dust? Do they really bother people? Is this a problem you need to solve? The ad doesn't say.

More Ways That Ads Convince You

- **Snob appeal:** A product is connected with being wealthy or famous.

- **Cause and effect:** Using a product will solve a problem or make your troubles go away.

- **Testimonial:** Someone talks about the benefits of the product based on his or her personal experience with it.

- **Bandwagon:** Peer pressure is used to convince buyers that "everyone is doing it."

- **Plain folks:** A product is connected with everyday people or common experiences.

- **Emotional appeal:** A product is linked with emotions, such as fear or happiness.

CHAPTER 3

Avoiding Unexpected Costs

Kayla bought a new showerhead and faucet for her bathtub. Then she called a plumber to install these new fixtures. The plumber gave her a written *estimate.* It stated that the job would cost about $160 in labor.

After agreeing to the price, Kayla signed the estimate. This *authorized* the plumber to do the work.

Estimate

A judgment of the cost or value of something. It's best to get estimates in writing.

Authorize

To give official permission to.

When the job was done, the plumber handed Kayla a bill for $479.50. She was shocked! That was nearly three times the amount of the estimate.

What Went Wrong?

Kayla did not carefully read the paper she signed. But by signing it, she authorized the plumber to do any extra work he felt was needed.

The plumber believed Kayla's old pipes wouldn't fit her new bathroom fixtures. So, he charged her extra for replacing the old pipes. He also charged her for removing and replacing several tiles around the bathtub.

Kayla didn't think the extra work was needed. But she had to pay the bill anyway. There was nothing else she could do.

How Can You Protect Yourself?

Has a similar situation ever happened to you? Can you think of ways to avoid such expensive surprises? Follow these tips:

→ Always get more than one estimate for a job. Repair people usually give estimates for free. If they want to charge you for an estimate, don't use them. Kayla should have asked at least one other plumber for an estimate. Another plumber might have warned her about matching new fixtures to old pipes.

→ Before you sign an agreement, make sure you know what it says. Because once you've signed it, you've authorized the work to be done. You might want to change the agreement before you sign it. Kayla could have written something like this on the plumbing estimate: "Further authorization needed if charges will be more than $250."

→ If you're having parts replaced, ask to see the old parts. That way, you can make sure the new parts were really put in place. Kayla should have asked to see the old pipes to prove that they were taken out.

→ Find out whether the repairs were done with new or rebuilt parts. Some things can be repaired with used parts that have been fixed up or redone. Rebuilt parts are cheaper than new parts, and some are just as good. Ask about using rebuilt parts ahead of time. And be sure to check the bill you get after the work's done. If the repair service said they'd use rebuilt parts, make sure you don't pay for new parts. Also make sure you're not getting rebuilt parts if you're being charged for new parts.

→ Be on the lookout for *fraud.* Report any repair person or fix-it service that cheats you. Your state's consumer protection agency may be able to help you get your money back. You'll need to have copies of your estimate and bill to prove you were cheated.

Fraud

Something that's done to trick or cheat someone out of money. In most cases, fraud involves a lie or some other kind of dishonesty.

Tips for Finding Good Repair People

1. Ask friends, neighbors, co-workers, and family members whom they use.

2. Interview at least three people, no matter how small the job is.

3. See if any complaints have been filed against these people about their work. Check with your state's consumer protection agency.

4. For each person, get the names and phone numbers of at least three earlier customers. Call and ask questions about the quality of the work the person did.

5. Get at least three estimates of the cost.

6. Trust your feelings. Don't hire someone that makes you uncomfortable.

Consumer Protection Agencies

Every state has a consumer protection agency or office of consumer affairs. So does the US government. What do these agencies do?

- Enforce laws that protect consumers
- Provide licenses for doing certain jobs
- Tell consumers about their rights
- Help consumers avoid unfair practices
- Help settle consumer complaints about poor work or service

Go to Court!

What if the carpenter you hired to do some repairs doesn't finish the job? And what if you keep calling him to ask about the work, but he never answers the phone or calls you back?

Many people with problems like this go to small claims court. This court is the lowest-level court in most states. It handles disagreements that involve small amounts of money—usually $1,500 or less. Each person in the disagreement presents his or her side of the issue. Attorneys aren't needed. A judge listens to each person's story and then makes a decision.

Chapter **4**

Searching for Bargains

A *bargain* is a good deal. Getting a bargain usually means buying a high-quality item for well below the usual cost. For smart shoppers, getting a bargain makes all their work worthwhile.

Learn the Language of Bargain Shopping

Paying a low price doesn't always mean you're getting a bargain. Sometimes, the price is low because the quality is low.

Look for these words to make sure you know what you're buying:

→ **"Irregular" or "Flawed":** If you see either of these words on a label, it means the product isn't quite perfect. It probably works just fine, but it may not look brand new. Depending on what the product is, its appearance may not matter to you.

→ **"As is":** This also means the product isn't perfect. It may have a small scratch or stain. An "as is" item of clothing may be missing a button or have a torn seam. An "as is" product may work just fine but not look the best.

If you buy something that's flawed, irregular, or "as is," you're accepting its less-than-perfect quality. This means that after you buy it, you probably won't be able to return it.

Also learn about kinds of stores that provide bargains:

→ **Outlet stores** sell well-known brands at greatly reduced prices. Outlet stores are often grouped in areas to form outlet malls.

→ A **factory outlet** sells items made by one company.

→ A **retail outlet** sells items that didn't sell at a department store.

Finding Used Bargains

Bargain hunters save millions of dollars a year by shopping for used items. Many used items are in good shape. Even so, make sure to look them over carefully before buying them. You usually can't return used items.

Where can you find used items?

Consignment Stores and Thrift Shops

Use online **directories** and the Yellow
Pages to find stores that sell used items.
Look especially for consignment stores
and thrift shops:

→ **Consignment shops** often have high-
  quality used furniture and clothing.
  Individuals bring their used items to these shops. When the items
  sell, the individuals get some of the money. You can find great
  bargains at these stores.

→ **Thrift shops** also sell used items. Usually, individuals donate these
  items, giving them to the shop for free. The money thrift shops
  make often supports a charity, such as a hospital or church. Some
  shops have "half-price days" or special bargain days.

Tips for Bargain Hunters

- Collect coupons and keep them organized. Carry them with you
  in a small envelope or billfold.
- Join online groups for bargain shoppers. Look at the offers they
  send you for local shops and restaurants.
- Find a grocery store that has "double-coupon days." Look at your
  grocery's weekly ad to see what's on sale.
- Join a wholesale shopping club, such as Sam's Club or Costco. An
  annual fee of $40 or $50 is usually required for an individual to join.
- Shop at outlet stores. Know the locations of outlet stores that
  sell the brands of products you like.

Classified Ads

You can also find terrific bargains by reading the **classified** ads online or in the newspaper. Keep in mind that the prices in classified ads aren't always firm. And some ads say "OBO," which stands for "or best offer." This means the seller might sell the item for less. If you offer a lower price and the seller accepts, you can save even more money.

Estate Sales, Bazaars, and Benefit Sales

Some classified ads tell about estate sales and bazaars or benefit sales:

→ An **estate sale** sells items from someone's home, often after he or she has died. Household items and furniture are often good bargains at estate sales.

→ **Bazaars and benefit sales** are held to raise money for charities, schools, and other good causes. At these sales, people donate crafts, food, and all sorts of used items to be sold at bargain rates.

Directory

A book or Web site that lists the names, addresses, and phone numbers of people, businesses, and organizations. A telephone book is an example of a directory.

Classified

Arranged in groups or by types. *Classified ads* group types of products, such as cars, furniture, and sports equipment.

Garage Sales and More!

Garage sales and yard sales are good places to find bargains, too. They often take place on weekends. Sometimes, many families get together and have a neighborhood garage sale.

Flea markets and swap meets are a lot like giant garage sales. They're usually held every weekend in large outdoor areas, such as fairgrounds and parking lots. Anyone may reserve a spot to sell new or used items.

Shopping with Online Classified Ads

Online ads are posted on Web sites. The sites are locally based, usually around large cities. Some sites target rural areas or offer specific types of items. Here are some popular sites:

BackPage.com	Sell.com
Craigslist.org	Facebook.com/marketplace
Oodle.com	Usfreeads.com
Kijiji.com	Stumblehere.com
Hoobly.com	

People who use online ads must follow the rules and guidelines of the Web site. For instance, there may be rules about how many ads one person can put on the site. If you shop at online sites, be careful not to become a victim of fraud. Never give out your full name, your address, or your Social Security or bank account number.

What Are Online Auctions?

At an *auction,* each item that's offered for sale is sold to the highest bidder. In other words, the item goes to the person who offers to pay the most for it. In an online auction, you go to a Web site and look at what items are for sale. If you find something you'd like to buy, you put in a bid. If you end up getting the item, the seller will make arrangements to send it to you.

Here are some well-known online auction sites:

eBay.com   Amazon.com   Yahoo.com

Tips for Shopping Online Auctions

- Read the description of the item you're interested in. Send questions to the seller using e-mail.

- Check the seller's history at the Web site. Find out whether anyone has complained about him or her.

- Check the cost of shipping. Some sellers charge extra to make more money.

- Don't bid on something if you don't trust the seller.

- Compare the prices of the same or similar items being sold by other people.

- To top other people's bids, go up pennies at a time.

- Pay for what you buy using a credit card. Don't pay with cash, check, or money order.

- Never give out your Social Security or bank account number.

Shopping for Goods

Shopping doesn't always mean buying things for fun! Sometimes, it means buying household items, such as a refrigerator or mattress. And sometimes, it means buying clothes for work. When you shop for goods like these, you want to get the most for your money. To do that, you need to explore all your options. That includes both new and used goods, as well as items available online and in catalogs.

Getting Started

Jamal was excited about his new job. He started in two weeks. But before he went to work, he had a lot to do.

Taking the job meant moving to a new city. Jamal had already rented an apartment there. It wasn't fancy, but he liked it. It would be great to have his own place, he thought.

There was just one problem: Jamal didn't really have anything to put in the apartment. He'd lived at his family's home until just after high school. And after that, he'd shared a house with some friends. He owned a bed, a small TV, and some towels.

Jamal was in a similar situation with clothing. Most of his clothes were those of a student, not someone who worked in an office. He couldn't afford to buy a closet full of new clothes. Even so, he'd need a few things to get started.

Before deciding what clothes he needed, Jamal looked over the clothes he already had. He had a few things he could wear to work. After looking through a catalog, he ordered a few more things. He chose basic styles and colors. They would be easy to match with other clothes—now and later.

Next, Jamal made a list of the household goods he needed. He knew he could get some of them from his family. His parents had old furniture in the basement, including a dresser and a table and chairs. Jamal wouldn't have picked out these things to buy at a store. But knowing what furniture costs, he was happy to have these used pieces. They'd get him started in his new home!

Return Policies

Most stores will let you return something that's defective, or faulty. When you return something that doesn't work, you may have three choices:

1. **Exchange:** You can exchange the item for another one.

2. **Store credit:** You can get something else at that store for the same price.

3. **Refund:** You can get your money back, which is a cash refund. Or you can have the refund applied to your debit card or credit card.

But what if you buy something and decide later that you don't want it? Can you exchange or return the item for a refund?

Guidelines for Making Returns

Often, you can return something you don't want. But you should follow these guidelines:

→ Return the item soon after you purchase it. Don't wait longer than a week.

→ Bring your receipt with you. It proves that you purchased the item. Having the receipt is the key to a problem-free return.

→ Bring the original packaging or box. Also bring the sales tag, instructions, and all other materials that came with the item.

→ Return the item to the customer service department at the store where you made the purchase. Some chain stores let customers return items at any of their *branches,* but many don't.

Branches

Stores that are part of the same chain, or group.

Making Illegal Returns

Returning items under false conditions is a type of theft. How is this crime committed?

- By stealing something from a store and then returning it without a receipt.
- By paying for something using a stolen check or credit card.
- By buying an item and planning to return it after using it.
- By changing the receipt to make the price higher and then returning the item for a refund.

→ If you paid by debit or credit card, bring it with you. The store will need your card to exchange or refund the purchase.

Return Policies Vary

Before you buy, know the store's return *policy.* Stores usually post their policies where you can see them— usually, near the cash register.

Policy
A plan or rule for how something will be done.

Here are some examples of return policies and what they mean:

→ **"A complete refund for any reason."** You'll almost certainly get your money back.

→ **"Returns only in exchange for other merchandise."** The store will give you a store credit or exchange the item for another one like it. You won't get your money back.

Merchandise

Items that are sold in a store. Merchandise is sometimes called *products* or *goods*.

Stricter Return Policies

To prevent illegal returns, many stores have changed their return policies. Most stores have made their policies tougher:

- Most stores no longer make promises like "100% satisfaction or you get your money back."
- Most stores will offer an exchange or store credit but not a refund.
- If the item has gone on sale by the time it's returned, the store might not take it back. If it does, you might get credit only for the sale amount.
- Many stores have shortened the period when they will accept returns. In most cases, you must return something within 30 days of buying it.

- **"No returns of any kind."** Stores that sell used or discounted items usually have a "No return" policy. You'll be stuck with anything you buy.

Nonreturnable Items

Most stores refuse to allow customers to return these items:

- **Food and other perishables** (items that spoil or don't stay fresh): The only exception might be an item that was already spoiled when you purchased it.

- **Items purchased for big discounts:** This includes sale items that are tagged "As is," "All sales final," or "No returns."

- **Items that have been used or damaged:** Stores can't resell these items and so won't take them back.

- **Personal items:** Items such as underwear and makeup can't be returned because of health reasons.

How Returns Drive Up Prices

Stores lose money when they take back merchandise. A large store or chain of stores can lose millions of dollars a year by accepting returned items. And in 2010, the cost of illegal returns was almost $14 billion.

   To make up for these losses, stores raise the prices of what they sell. Store managers look at sales records to figure out how much money is lost to returns. They figure out what percentage of earnings is lost every year. Then they raise prices to cover that loss. And of course, consumers pay the extra cost.

CHAPTER **2**

Buying Household Goods

Imagine that you're moving into your own apartment. When you walk through the door, you see empty rooms, bare walls, and lots of empty cupboards. Now, it's up to you to furnish the rooms and fill the shelves.

You probably can't afford to buy everything all at once. So, where do you start?

List Your Needs

First, make a list of the things you need most. Begin with basic furniture, such as a bed, a table, and chairs. Next, list small household items, such as pots and pans, towels, and sheets.

Then, consider your **appliance** needs. Will you need to get a TV? A toaster? An iron? A microwave oven?

Set Your Priorities

After you've made your list, decide which items you need right away. Label those items with a number 1. Then label the other items in order of their importance—2, 3, 4, and so on.

As you're labeling items, you're thinking through your **priorities.** The number-1 items are your top priorities. A bed, for example, is more important than a bookshelf. Once you've set your priorities, you'll know what to buy now and what to buy later.

Appliance

A piece of equipment designed to do a certain job or task. Many common appliances are in the kitchen, such as refrigerators, dishwashers, and stoves.

Priority

Something of greatest importance or concern.

New or Used?

Think about how to save money on your top-priority items. Also think about which items to buy new versus used. Use these tips to help you decide:

→ Buying used furniture will save a lot of money. Check classified ads, estate sales, garage sales, and flea markets.

→ For health reasons, it's best to purchase a brand-new mattress. But look for a used box spring and bed frame.

→ Many household items, such as pots and pans, can also be purchased used. Look for them at thrift stores, estate sales, and garage sales.

→ Your family and friends may have household items they don't use. To help you get started, they might give these items to you or sell them for very little.

Goodwill Stores

Are you looking for bargains on household items? A good place to start is your local Goodwill store. Goodwill Industries International has the goal of helping people in need find opportunities. Helping people reach their goals also helps them contribute to their communities. At a Goodwill store, you can find all kinds of used household items. The items have been donated to Goodwill and then cleaned or fixed up. They are sold at bargain prices. At Goodwill Outlet stores, you buy goods by the pound, which is even cheaper.

Tips for Buying Appliances

→ It's usually best to buy appliances new. The store will repair them or take them back if they don't work.

→ Avoid expensive features you don't need. Must your TV have a flat screen? Does it need to have a built-in DVD player? Extras add a lot to the basic price. Decide which features you really need before you go shopping.

→ Make sure the appliance is "user friendly." Don't buy something you won't be able to use.

Should You Repair or Replace an Appliance?

Every appliance breaks down at some point. Then, you have to decide whether to repair it or replace it. Here's how to decide:

- If you paid less than $150 for the appliance replace it. Buying a new appliance will be cheaper than repairing the old one.

- If the cost of repairs is more than half the price of buying new, then replace the appliance.

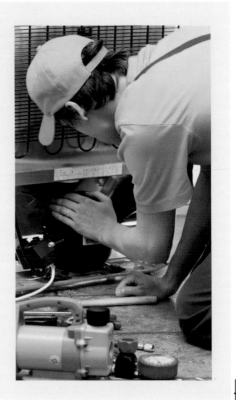

→ To make sure appliances are really new, look them over before you buy. Check for scratches and dents. Check the box. Is it properly packed? Are the parts sealed? Does the model number on the box match the one on the appliance? Does the **warranty** cover immediate repairs? If not, the item may not be new.

→ Look for an *R, B,* or *X* scratched on the back of the appliance. If you find one, the appliance is likely a rebuilt product.

> **Warranty**
>
> A written promise or contract about a product's quality. A warranty usually offers to repair or replace a product that is faulty.

[FACT]

Average Lifetimes of Major Appliances

Clothes dryer:	Microwave oven:
13 years	9 years
Clothes washer (front loading):	Oven (single, slide-in):
11 years	17 years
Clothes washer (top loading):	Refrigerator (compact):
14 years	5 years
Cooktop (single, built-in):	Refrigerator (one-door):
13 years	19 years
Dishwasher (built-in):	Refrigerator (side-by-side):
13 years	14 years
Garbage disposal (in sink):	Room air conditioner:
12 years	12 years

CHAPTER **3**

Assembling a Wardrobe

Your **lifestyle** determines the kind of **wardrobe** you need. Think about your usual activities. The clothes you wear most often should be your first priority. Next, think about what you do the rest of the time. Clothes for these activities should be your second priority.

For example, Leo is a student with a part-time job. What kind of clothes should he buy first: clothes for fun, work, or school? What kind of clothes should be Leo's second priority?

Lifestyle
The way someone lives. A person's lifestyle usually reflects his or her values and attitudes.

Wardrobe
A person's complete collection of clothes.

Tips for Building a Wardrobe

→ Make a list of what you need before you shop for clothes.

→ Stick to your priorities. Otherwise, you may waste money on things you don't really need.

→ Buy good-quality clothes that will last. It's better to have a few well-made pieces of clothing than lots of clothes that will wear out fast.

→ Choose basic styles you can make formal or informal for different activities.

→ Avoid paying a lot of money for trendy clothes that will soon go out of style.

→ Choose new clothes that go with clothes you already have. Try to create at least three new outfits from each new item you buy.

→ Buy clothes for comfort and fit. You won't want to wear clothes that pinch or bind. And you won't look good in them, either.

→ Read the fabric labels of clothes before you buy them. Check to see what kind of cleaning and care they will need. Avoid buying clothes that wrinkle easily or have to be dry cleaned. Some dry-cleaned clothes can be washed by hand.

- Remove stains right away. If left untreated, they can become *permanent*.

- Take time to change into old clothes for play, housework, and messy jobs. Wear an apron when cooking.

- Shop for clothes at discount stores and outlets.

Permanent

Lasting forever or unable to be changed.

How to Recognize Good Quality

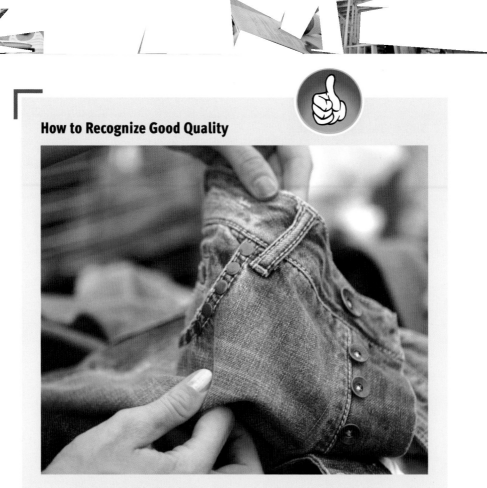

- **Cloth:** Look for fabric that flows and drapes nicely. Also look for even color and weaving. Look for patterns such as stripes and plaids to line up.

- **Seams:** Turn the garment inside out. Look at the seams, which is where the pieces are sewn together. Check for straight, tight seams, with no loose threads. Check that the ends of seams are secure.

- **Closures:** Make sure zippers, buttons, and other fasteners are secure and work properly.

- **Fit:** Try on the item. Does it hang and fit well? Does it suit your body, coloring, and style?

Smart Buys in Clothing

What items of clothing are worth spending more on to get good quality?

- Shoes, belts, and handbags in neutral colors that you can mix and match.
- Clothes you can dress up or down, such as plain black pants or a basic black dress.
- Classic styles, fabrics, and colors that will stay in fashion.
- Clothes that fit well and flatter you.
- Items that you will wear often.

Tips for Clothing Care

- Wash clothes only when necessary.
- Hang items on the line to dry.
- Iron only if needed.
- Hang clothes on good-quality hangers in an uncrowded space.
- Fix tears, ripped seams, and loose buttons right away, before they get worse.
- Treat stains with stain or spot remover. Then wash the item immediately in cold water. Repeat if necessary. (Hot water and hot dryers can set a stain, making it permanent.)
- Wear old, worn clothes when doing dirty jobs.
- Follow the care instructions on clothing labels.

CHAPTER **4**

Shopping from Home

Few things are as convenient as shopping from home. Millions of people buy things from catalogs, on the Internet, or by phone.

Advantages of Shopping from Home

→ You can shop any time you want, day or night. And there's no traffic, crowds, or waiting in line for service.

→ You can find anything you want, new or used. And you can get things from *marketplaces* all around the world.

→ You can often get great prices. This is especially true if you buy direct from a factory or a discount warehouse.

Marketplace

An area in a town or city where people come to buy and sell things.

Why Shop Online?

By 2014, online retail sales are expected to reach $249 billion. Consumers will make 1 in 12 purchases online. Online retail is especially strong for clothes, shoes, and accessories.

And why do people like to shop online?

- Checking prices from one retailer to another is easier on computer than on foot.

- Reading about product features is fast and easy online.

- Most online retailers can tell you whether they have the item you want in stock.

- Most merchandise can be ordered online and shipped, saving you a trip to the store.

- In some cases, shipping is free.

Disadvantages of Shopping from Home

→ Because it's so convenient, you may buy more things than you need or can afford.

→ You'll often pay extra to have your purchases shipped to you. (Look for retailers that offer free shipping.)

→ You must rely on *descriptions* and pictures of the products you buy. You can't actually inspect or try what you're buying until it arrives.

Description

A detailed explanation of what someone or something is like. A description can include sights, sounds, and smells.

→ If you're unhappy with what you buy, you'll have to ship it back. That means paying a return shipping fee. Also, some companies charge a restocking fee for putting returned items back on the shelves. Avoid doing business with companies that charge this kind of fee.

→ You can spend a lot of time shopping online!

Placing an Order

→ Keep records of all the orders you place. Print out copies of the order form and other paperwork you fill out.

→ Be sure to fill out the order form completely. Look for the following sections:

- The abbreviation *Qty* stands for *Quantity* on many order forms. Be sure to write down how many of each item you want to order.

- The word *Code* usually means the style or model number. You'll find the code number beside the product description.

- The *Unit Price* is the cost of one item.

→ See what options are available for shipping. Keep in mind that the faster the method of shipping, the more it costs. Also check whether free shipping is available.

→ Deal only with well-known stores and Web sites that have good return policies. Use the ***toll-free*** 800 phone number to call and ask questions. Don't use 900 numbers. They cost money.

→ Never pay for the order with cash. If you can, use a credit card. Doing so gives you added protection if you have a problem with your order.

Toll-free

Not requiring payment of a fee for use. Calling a toll-free telephone number allows making long-distance calls free of charge.

Tips for Safe Online Shopping

- Shop only from online stores you trust. Learn about unfamiliar stores at the Better Business Bureau (www.bbb.org/us).

- When you check out, look for security signs. Those signs include an unbroken lock or key, the words *Secure Sockets Layer (SSL),* and an address bar that begins with *https.*

- Check the store's privacy statement. It will tell you how your personal information will be used. If you can't find a privacy statement, don't shop at the store.

- Pay with a credit card. If anything goes wrong with your purchase, you'll be protected.

- Save or print out all records of the purchase.

Tips for Protecting Your Online Identity

- Most online stores require you to create an account. When you do, choose a login and password very carefully. Choose a password that you will remember but that no one else will guess.

- Never provide personal information using e-mail. It doesn't have security features to block others from getting the information.

- After you order something, you might receive an e-mail request for personal information. Ignore and delete it. Criminals sometimes use e-mail to trick people into giving out their user IDs, passwords, credit card numbers, and Social Security numbers.

Shopping for Services

Another kind of shopping involves buying services, such as life insurance, cable TV, and home repair work. Paying for these services can be expensive. In some cases, you make monthly payments for years. In other cases, you pay for work that you expect to last a long time. To spend your money wisely, you should shop around for professional services. Learn how to find the best quality and the best price available.

Making Smart Decisions

Maria and her mother could hardly believe it: They owned a house! Buying it had meant years of cutting expenses and saving money. And today at the bank, they'd signed what seemed a hundred different forms. But after they'd finished, the house was theirs.

Both women had lots of ideas for fixing the place up. It needed some work, for sure. They planned on doing certain things themselves, such as painting and yard work. But they knew they'd need to hire people to do other projects.

One of those projects was to remodel the bathroom. Maria and her mother had talked to several professional services about doing the work. Maria thought it was important to get several opinions of the time and cost needed for the project. Then, she and her mother would decide which service to hire.

Maria had also talked to the local cable TV company about setting up service. She was surprised to learn that she could get TV, telephone,

and Internet service from the same company. The house had never been wired for cable TV. That meant some extra work would be needed. But because Maria was a new customer, some of the work would be done for free.

Something else Maria and her mother planned to check into was life insurance. If something happened to one of them, the other couldn't afford to keep the house. Buying life insurance would protect them from losing something they'd worked really hard to get.

Checking Out Reputations and References

From time to time, everyone needs the help of a professional service to take care of a problem. A *professional* is someone who's trained and experienced in doing a particular kind of work. Examples include carpenters, plumbers, and electricians, as well as tailors and seamstresses, gardeners and lawn care workers.

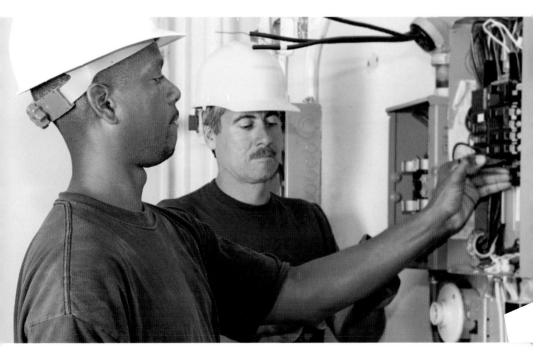

Choose a Professional Service

How should you choose a professional service? Shop for it, just like you'd shop for anything else. First, consider your needs. Then, look for people who can do the job right. Finally, compare prices.

Professional services that do repair work must pass state tests and be licensed. If a service is licensed, its license number is often shown in ads in the phone book or newspaper or on its Web site. Having a license doesn't prove that a service is honest or gives the best prices. But it does usually mean that the service's workers are experienced.

Get Referrals and References

Many professional services that do repairs are known for doing good work at honest prices. They have a good *reputation,* which means others think highly of them.

How can you find out which services have a good reputation? Ask family members, friends, and anyone else you trust for **referrals.** Whom have they hired that they would **recommend?** Also ask whom they would *not* recommend, based on their experiences.

Contact the professional services that others have recommended to you. Ask what they charge and when they're available to work. Also ask each service for three **references.** Call those people and ask about the quality of work the service did for them.

Is Your Professional Service Licensed?

There are two main benefits to hiring a service that's licensed:

1. You can trust that the workers have the skills, knowledge, and experience needed to do a good job.
2. You will be protected from paying extra charges if something goes wrong. The state office that issued the license will help you solve any disagreements with the service.

Before you hire a professional service, ask to see its license. Find out what office issued the license and contact it. Ask these questions:

- Does the service have a current license?
- How long has the service been licensed?
- Was the license ever taken away? If so, why and for how long?

Get Estimates

Also ask each professional service for a free, written estimate. Each estimate should give you a good idea of the following:

1. What work needs to be done.

2. How long the work will take.

3. When the work will begin and end.

4. About how much the work will cost.

Ask questions. Make sure you understand the work that's needed before you hire a service to do it. Tell each professional service that you'll be in touch when you've made your decision. Take your time. Never agree to anything that you don't understand, want, or need.

Referral

A suggestion of someone to contact to provide a service.

Recommend

To suggest that something is a good idea.

References

People who are willing to give their opinions about someone else's work, based on their experience with him or her.

Use Your Own Judgment

Don't hire the professional service with the lowest estimate just because it's the lowest. Cost isn't everything. Instead, choose a service that does these things:

→ Takes time to explain the job in a way you understand.

→ Makes suggestions that could save you money.

→ Guarantees its work (promises 100 percent satisfaction or your money back).

→ Has accident insurance for the worker who does repairs in your home.

→ Has been in business a long time and can name satisfied customers.

Questions to Ask References

• Was the job done on time and on budget? If not, why?

• Was the job done well? If not, why?

• Did the worker treat the property and family members with respect?

• Did the worker clean up after himself or herself?

• How well did the worker communicate about what needed to be done?

• Were there any problems? If so, how were they solved?

Stay away from services that do these things:

→ Charge for giving you an estimate. (Estimates should be free.)

→ Demand payment before the work is finished or ask to be paid in cash. (Both suggest the service isn't honest.)

→ Won't accept payment on a credit card. (Your credit card company can help protect you from having to pay for poor service.)

How Much Should Repair Work Cost?

Rates can vary widely among professional services. So, before you hire a service, consider these guidelines:

- **Qualifications:** The more training and experience workers have, the higher the rate.

- **Basic rate:** Some services charge by the hour. Often, the first hour costs more. Other services charge a flat fee for a certain kind of job.

- **Scheduling:** Doing a big job or several small jobs at once can cost less per hour than a small job.

- **Parts and materials:** The cost of any parts and materials needed will be added to your bill.

- **Travel:** Many services charge for travel time. This charge is often called a *trip fee*.

CHAPTER **2**

Comparing Life Insurance Policies

Jason has a wife and two children. They are his **_dependents._** To protect them in case something happened to him, Jason bought a $200,000 life insurance policy. He named his wife and children as his **_beneficiaries._**

If Jason dies, his wife and children will get the money from this policy. They'll get $200,000 to help make up for Jason's lost income. That's what life insurance does: It provides money to someone's beneficiaries after he or she has died.

Who Needs Life Insurance?

Does part of your income help support other people? If so, then having life insurance is a good idea. Here are some people who should think about buying life insurance:

- Parents with children who don't yet support themselves.
- Someone whose husband or wife either doesn't work or works part time.
- Someone who has large bank loans or owes money to credit card companies.
- Someone who takes care of an aging or disabled relative or friend who couldn't afford to hire someone else.

Dependent

Someone who's supported financially by someone else. Children are dependents of their parents.

Beneficiary

Someone who benefits from something. In the case of life insurance, the beneficiary is the person who will receive the money paid by the policy.

Paying Premiums

To pay for life insurance, you have to make regular payments called *premiums.* If you miss a payment, your policy could *lapse.* If that happens, you might lose your insurance and all the premiums you've already paid.

What if you can't afford life insurance premiums and you don't have dependents? Life insurance may not be important for you. But if you do need life insurance, it's wise to compare premiums from different companies.

Premiums

The fees paid to have an insurance policy. Most premiums are paid at regular times, such as monthly or annually.

Insurance Company Ratings

Avoid life insurance deals that are offered by mail, over the phone, or on TV. Shop around for insurance companies that have A or A+ ratings. These companies will most likely be in business and be able to pay

off your policy in the future, if needed.

Your public librarian can help you look up companies with good ratings. You can also find this information online.

The Cost of Life Insurance

A number of things about you will determine what you pay:

- **Age:** The younger you are, the lower your monthly premium will be.

- **Health:** The better your physical health, the less you'll pay. Some insurance companies also consider risk factors, such as your family's health history. It helps to have healthy parents and grandparents.

- **Tobacco:** Nonsmokers pay less than smokers. People who smoke a little, who smoke cigars, or who use smokeless tobacco pay less.

- **Type of policy:** Whole-life insurance costs the most and is worth the most. For term insurance, the longer the time period covered, the greater the cost.

- **Insurance company:** Highly rated companies charge more. But you can also trust that they'll pay the benefits, when needed.

Types of Life Insurance

→ **Term insurance:** Term life insurance costs the least. Premiums vary by company and by the size of the policy. A $100,000 policy costs more than a $50,000 policy. Term insurance lasts for only a certain period of time. For example, it might be a 10-year policy. When the term is up, the policy ends. You don't get any money back. Usually, you can renew the policy, but the premiums will be higher. That's because you'll be older than you were 10 years ago. The older you are, the more it costs to buy life insurance.

→ **Whole-life insurance:** A whole-life policy lasts your entire life. Of course, you must keep paying the premiums. These monthly or yearly charges will be higher than those for term insurance. But the payments won't change, even as you get older. Whole-life insurance is sometimes called *straight life* or *permanent life* insurance.

Other Terms to Know

→ **Dividends:** After many years, some whole-life policies start to earn money. These earnings are called *dividends*. Many people use dividends to lower their premiums.

→ **Face value:** The *face value* is what the life insurance policy is worth. If you buy a $20,000 policy, the face value is $20,000. That's how much your beneficiaries would receive if you died.

→ **Cash value:** After many years, most whole-life policies have a certain *cash value*—say, $6,000 on a $50,000 policy. If you wanted that money, you could cash in the policy. You would no longer be protected by the life insurance, though.

How Much Life Insurance Do You Need?

1. Calculate the cost of your death: funeral costs, medical expenses, and estate taxes.

2. How much money do you owe? Include loans, credit cards, and so on.

3. How much income will your dependents need? Take your yearly earnings and multiply by the number of years until you retire at age 65.

4. Determine future expenses: maybe college for your children or what it would cost to hire people to do the tasks you do, such as child care or yard work.

5. Add up the amounts from steps 1–4.

6. Figure out your financial worth: savings, investments, retirement plans.

7. Determine how much your husband or wife might earn after you die.

8. Add the amounts from steps 6 and 7. Subtract this amount from the figure in step 5. This is a rough estimate of how much life insurance you need.

Chapter 3

Comparing Cable and Other Services

Cable TV service is provided by wires that run underground. If your home is wired for cable, you can get more channels than are available on **broadcast TV.** With many cable TV services, you can also get Internet and telephone service.

Cable TV service isn't free. You pay a monthly fee. And the more services you want, the more you'll pay. If you don't watch much TV or rarely use the Internet at home, cable service may not be worth paying for. But for most people, cable service is a basic monthly expense.

Most communities get cable TV service from one company. So, if you aren't happy with the service, there's not much you can do.

Guidelines for Getting Cable TV

→ **Plan ahead before having cable installed.** Keep in mind that you'll be charged for each service visit from the cable company. To keep costs down, have as much done in one visit as possible. Here are some services you might have to pay for:

- Your entire home or some of its rooms may need to be wired.

- You'll need at least one converter box to connect your TV to cable.

- You may want extra outlets (connection plugs) so you can watch cable TV in different rooms or on more than one TV.

- You may need to connect your DVD or DVR (digital video recorder) to the new system.

- If you want Internet service, you'll need a cable modem or a Wi-Fi router.

Broadcast TV
Television programming that's transmitted over the airwaves, not via cable or satellite. Broadcast TV is sometimes called *network TV*.

Install
To set something up and make it ready for use.

→ **Look for free installation offers and special rates.** Cable companies often offer special deals to get new customers. Check online for specials. Your local cable company may offer a free self-installation kit. Or you may have to sign up for a *trial offer,* where you try something like a pay movie channel for a short period of time. It may be worth it, if the cost of the trial offer is less than the installation fee. When the trial period ends, remember to cancel the pay movie channel.

→ **Choose your services wisely.** What services do you need? Ask your cable company about special prices or bundled plans of services. *Bundled plans* provide two or more services, such as TV, Internet, and telephone. The price is usually discounted from the cost of buying the services separately. Some cable companies have reduced prices for bundled plans for new customers. But make sure you understand what the long-term cost will be. Also check prices before you sign up for different *subscription* packages, such as movie and sports channels. Some are quite expensive. Again, cable companies may offer deals to new customers. But find out what the cost will be after the deal has run out.

→ **Think about satellite TV.**
Satellite TV is different from cable. Satellite TV uses a small dish to capture TV signals from satellites. Check your local satellite companies for rates. They may offer special deals for new customers, like cable companies do. They may also offer service bundles. Do a little research to see which service might work best for you: cable or satellite.

→ **Pay your bills on time.**
Cable and satellite TV companies charge fees for late payments and returned checks. And if you don't pay your bill, you may even lose your service.

Subscription

An agreement to pay for and receive something over a period of time. Magazines can be bought and received with subscriptions.

Choosing a Bundled Plan

- **In general:** Don't buy a plan that has more than you need. Do you want TV, phone, and Internet? Just two? Just one?

- **For phone service:** Do you make long-distance calls? Do you talk the most during the day, evening, or night? Will you use call waiting, call forwarding, and voice mail?

- **For TV:** How many channels do you want? Do you have high-definition (HD) TV? Will you use a digital video recorder (DVR) to record movies and TV shows?

- **For Internet:** Do you need a fast connection to download large files or play games? Do you rarely go online or just need to check e-mail? Do you want Wi-Fi? Do you already have cable service?

What Is Wi-Fi?

Wi-Fi is a wireless network for computers and mobile digital devices, such as smartphones and iPads. It allows computers and devices to connect to the Internet without an electrical cord. Like cell phones, TVs, and radios, Wi-Fi transmits signals across the airwaves. All that's needed is a Wi-Fi receiver, which is sometimes called an *access point* or *hot spot*. Receivers can be found in many public places, including libraries, airports, and coffee shops. You can also set up a receiver quickly and easily in your home.

Tips for Safe Wi-Fi Use

Wi-Fi gives you the freedom to use your computer wherever you want. But with that freedom comes greater risk to your security and privacy. Theft of personal data is a serious risk with Wi-Fi. How can you protect yourself?

- Keep your computer updated with the latest versions of software. This includes your operating system, Web browser, and different kinds of security programs.

- Set up your computer so you have to select a Wi-Fi network before connecting. Don't let the computer select one for you.

- Never connect to an unknown Wi-Fi network.

- Don't do online banking, make online purchases, use e-mail, or send instant messages on an open (unsecured) network.

- Never enter a password or account numbers on a Web page that's not protected. Look for *https* in the address bar.

- Turn off Wi-Fi on your computer when you're not online.

Chapter 4

Hiring a Professional versus Doing It Yourself

Sometimes, it's worth it to hire a professional to perform a service for you. And sometimes, it pays to do the job yourself.

Making this decision depends on what work needs to be done and what kinds of skills you have. You can waste money trying to repair something that's beyond your ability. In fact, you could easily make the problem worse. Then, it might cost you three times as much to get the problem fixed by a professional.

When to Hire a Professional

You should hire a pro, rather than do the job yourself, if any of the following is possible:

→ Making a mistake could lead to a bigger problem or even create a **disaster.**

→ You could fall, get an electric shock, or be hurt in some way.

→ The job requires handling poisons or toxic materials.

Disaster
A damaging or harmful event.

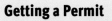

[FACT]

Getting a Permit

Some jobs require getting a permit to make sure work is done safely. For instance, a permit is usually needed if the structure of the building is being changed. A permit is also likely needed for work on a mechanical system, such as heating or cooling. Electrical and plumbing work usually require permits, too.

To find out if you need a permit, check with your city government. If a permit is needed, you'll have to pay for it. The fee will be based on the cost of your project. If you're supposed to get a permit but don't, you might have to pay a fine. Or you might lose your homeowner's insurance.

While the job is underway, you may be required to post the permit on the building. And after the job's been finished, you may be required to have the work inspected by the city.

→ Other people could be harmed by what you do.

→ The job requires professional training.

→ The job requires tools you don't have or don't know how to use.

How else can you avoid extra problems and costs when something needs repair?

→ If a product breaks, check the warranty. It may cover the cost of having repairs done by a professional. If you try to repair the item yourself, you could lose your warranty protection.

→ Never try to fix something that doesn't belong to you. Let the owner take care of the problem.

When to Do It Yourself

Lots of things are easy to fix. For example, you don't need a professional to change a light bulb or replace a drawer handle.

If you decide you're the person for the job, make sure you know what to do. Lots of good do-it-yourself information is available at the library and on the Internet.

Also make sure you know how to do the job safely. Here are some do-it-yourself safety tips:

→ Always keep safety in mind. Use **caution** and good judgment.

→ Make sure your work area has plenty of light, so you can see what you're doing.

→ Make sure the area has good **ventilation** when you're working with chemicals.

→ Read and follow all directions for product use. Pay particular attention to any warnings given on product labels.

Caution

Care taken to avoid damage, harm, or mistakes.

Ventilation

A supply of fresh and flowing air.

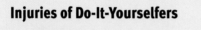

- → Read all instructions and warnings before using power tools.

- → Wear gloves, goggles, masks, and other protective clothing, as suggested by the warning labels.

- → Check out a ladder before you climb it. Make sure it's sturdy and safe. Follow the safety guidelines for using the ladder.

Injuries of Do-It-Yourselfers

Common Injuries

Cuts

Bruises

Sprains

Broken bones

Head injuries

Neck injuries

Eye injuries

Amputated (cut-off) fingers

Poisoning

Burns

Common Causes

- Falls from ladders and roofs
- Improper use of power tools (such as lawnmowers, nail guns, and power saws)
- Dangerous use or mixing of chemicals (paints, solvents, cleaners, gardening solutions)
- Failure to read and follow instructions

What Goes in a Basic Toolbox?

Claw hammer

Utility knife and extra blades

Tape measure (at least 12 feet)

Tape: duct, electrical, plumbing

Flashlight

Level

Set of pliers, including needle-
nose pliers

Wrenches: adjustable, crescent
set, Allen set

Screwdrivers: standard and
Phillips

Electric drill and drill bits

Selection of hardware: nails,
screws, washers, nuts, and
bolts

Consumer Rights

Not every purchase is a satisfying one, unfortunately. You've probably bought something that broke down or paid for a service you were unhappy with. Maybe you've even been taken advantage of by a dishonest business. Knowing your rights as a consumer will help you solve problems like these. And knowing about credit cards, warranties, and the like may help you avoid having the problems in the first place.

Knowing What to Do

It was Wednesday, Will's regular day off. And that afternoon, he made his weekly visit to see Grandma June. She always had lunch ready when he got there. And after they'd eaten, she usually had a few chores for him to do. He didn't mind the work, because he enjoyed spending time with his grandmother.

But today when Will arrived, lunch wasn't ready and Grandma June was upset. Just an hour earlier, a man had called and said he worked at her credit card company. He had some questions about her account, he'd said. Grandma hadn't asked for his name or phone number. But

he'd gotten a lot of information from her. She'd given him her credit card number and other important details.

After Grandma June got off the phone, she knew she'd made a mistake. She was embarrassed and worried. "I don't know what to do," she told Will.

Thankfully, Will knew what to do. He called the credit card company right away. He explained what had happened. Sure enough, someone had already started buying things with Grandma June's credit card!

The credit card company cancelled the card. And because the problem had been reported immediately, Grandma wouldn't be responsible for the charges.

Will had heard on the news about elderly people being victims of fraud. But he knew it could happen to anyone. Knowing your rights as a consumer was important at any age.

CHAPTER 1

Credit Card Benefits

Have you ever tried to rent a car without a credit card? It's nearly impossible. In fact, many businesses require having a credit card before they'll perform a service.

Protection for the Business

Having a customer's credit card protects a business. It *guarantees* that they'll be paid for the service they provide. It also guarantees they'll get paid for any extra costs involved. For instance, a car rental company wants to make sure it will get paid if a customer damages a car.

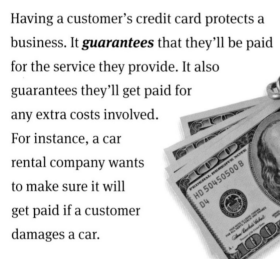

Guarantee

A promise of quality or responsibility.

Protection for You

Having a credit card can protect you, too. Suppose you feel you've been cheated by a business where you bought something with your credit card. Your credit card company will help you settle the problem.

First, report the problem to your credit card company immediately. Call and explain exactly what happened. Also explain that you plan to **dispute** paying for the product or service. Then, follow up your call with a letter to the credit card company.

Next, try to settle the problem with the business. You might need help from a consumer protection organization. You might even have to go to court.

Dispute

To challenge or disagree with. The word *dispute* can also be used to mean a disagreement.

All of these steps take time. But during that time, you won't be out any money. When your credit card bill arrives, you'll subtract the disputed amount from the total that's owed. Then you'll pay the rest of the bill or the amount that's required.

If you've reported the problem correctly, your credit card company won't make you pay the disputed charge. It won't make you pay other fees on the disputed balance, either. That includes the *interest,* which is the fee the lender charges.

Your Credit History

- **Why is your credit history important?** Your credit history is like a report card of how well you pay your bills. Banks and other lenders look at it to decide whether to lend you money—for instance, to buy a car. If you've never had a credit card or borrowed money, you won't have a credit history. And that means banks probably won't lend you money.

- **How can you build a good credit history?** Be responsible with your money. Start by getting a credit card from a store. Then each month, make your payment on time. Also pay your other bills on time and in full, as often as possible. If you've never had credit, making payments on time for one year will get you off to a good start. If you've been late with payments, it will take two years of paying on time to improve your credit.

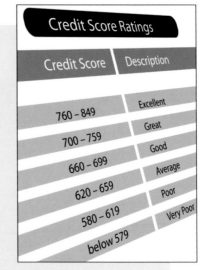

Credit Score Ratings

Credit Score	Description
760 – 849	Excellent
700 – 759	Great
660 – 699	Good
620 – 659	Average
580 – 619	Poor
below 579	Very Poor

Other Benefits of Credit Card Use

Using a credit card has other benefits, as well. But keep in mind that some are clearly better than others:

- **Cash advances:** Most credit cards let you get cash from a bank or ATM—no questions asked. Be aware, however, that this kind of loan is very expensive. You'll be charged high interest plus other fees. But in an emergency, having a quick way to get cash can be very helpful.

- **Rebates:** Some credit cards offer *rebates*, which gives you money back on all the purchases you make with the card. A rebate is usually a small percentage of the price. If you use your credit card to buy something expensive, like a refrigerator, you might earn a nice discount. But most rebates are worth only a few cents.

- **Extended warranties:** Many products have a warranty. That means the manufacturer guarantees the product will work and last for a certain time—say, 90 days. Some credit card companies offer to lengthen the time of the warranty. If you buy the product using your credit card, the warranty may be extended from 90 days to six months or a year.

- **Lost card coverage:** If your credit card is lost or stolen, call your credit card company immediately. Then follow up your call with a letter. If someone uses your card, you won't have to pay the charges. Under US law, if you report the loss immediately, you won't have to pay for more than $50 of the charges, if that.

Costs of Using Credit Cards

When you use a credit card, you're borrowing money. And that costs money! Here are some of the kinds of fees you may pay to use a credit card:

- **Monthly:** Every month, you'll make a minimum payment. You'll also pay interest on the *balance*, which is the total amount you owe.
- **Extras:** You'll be charged fees for paying late, for getting cash advances, and for going over the spending limit that's been set for you. Some cards also charge an annual fee.
- **Annual percentage rate (APR):** The APR is the interest charged on your balance. Some credit cards don't charge interest for the first few months, if you pay on time.

Remember: You can avoid many fees by paying your bill on time and in full.

Credit Cards versus Debit Cards

	Debit Card	Credit Card
Whose money am I spending?	Yours. You can't spend more than you have in your checking account.	Someone else's. You're borrowing money that you'll have to pay back.
Can I get this kind of card?	Most people can open a checking account and get a debit card.	You must have a fairly good credit history to get a credit card.
What's my spending limit?	The amount of money in your checking account. Some debit cards have a daily limit—usually, $1,000 to $3,000.	The amount is set by the credit card company based on your credit history. There's usually no daily limit.
Can I make cash withdrawals?	Yes. You can go to the bank or use an ATM. You may pay a fee, and you may be able to withdraw only $300 a day.	Yes. You can go to the bank or use an ATM. But you'll pay a high fee and a high interest rate on this money.

CHAPTER **2**

Making Complaints

You'd like to be satisfied with the goods and services you buy. And as a consumer, the law gives you the right to be satisfied. That's why you should always make a *complaint* if something goes wrong. You're legally *entitled* to a solution to the problem.

Complaint

A statement saying that something is unsatisfactory or unacceptable.

Entitled

Having the right to do something or receive something.

How to Make a Complaint

Most businesses will do their best to settle consumers' problems. If they don't, consumer protection agencies can help people get results.

If you have a consumer complaint, follow these steps to solve it:

1. **Explain the problem.** Be ready to explain what went wrong and why. Make a list of all the events that led up to the problem. Also list any other issues the problem has created.

2. **Decide how you'd like the problem to be solved.** Do you want an exchange? Do you want your money back? Do you want the work redone? You get to decide on an acceptable solution. It's your money.

[FACT]

Top-10 Areas of Consumer Complaints

1. **Cars:** Dishonesty by sellers, faulty repairs, leasing and towing disputes

2. **Credit/Debt:** Disputes over billing and fees, fraud with home loans, improper or illegal debt collection methods

3. **Home improvement/Construction:** Poor-quality work, failure to start or finish a job

4. **Phone, cable TV, electricity, heat, and other utilities:** Problems with service, disputes over billing

5. **Retail sale:** False advertising and other misleading methods, faulty merchandise, failure to deliver merchandise, problems with rebates, gift cards, and coupons

6. **Professional services:** Misleading practices, poor-quality work, failure to have required licenses, failure to complete work

7. **Internet sales:** Misleading practices, failure to deliver purchases made online

8. **Household goods:** Poor quality, misleading descriptions, failure to deliver, faulty repairs

9. (tie) **Landlords/Tenants:** Failure to make repairs or provide services, failure to pay rent and other fees, unhealthy and unsafe conditions

9. (tie) **Door-to-door, direct mail, and telephone sales:** Misleading practices, failure to deliver products, violations of "Do Not Call" law

10. **Health products and services:** Misleading information, failure to deliver products, unlicensed workers

3. **Gather your records.** You'll need receipts, bills, *cancelled checks,* estimates, and other records that back up your complaint. In some situations, you may want to take photographs. Never give anyone your original records. Make copies of all your records, in case you need them later.

4. **Decide what action to take.** If you bought a faulty product, take it back to the store and ask for a refund or exchange. You can also make a complaint to the manufacturer. If you're unhappy with a service you paid for, call the manager of the business. Explain what you want done. Sometimes, making a phone call can lead to a satisfactory solution.

Cancelled check

A check that's been paid by the bank. Banks send back cancelled checks to the person who wrote them or provide copies of the checks, if needed.

5. **Write a letter of complaint.** If you can't settle your complaint with a phone call or a visit, write a polite but firm letter. Your letter should do these things:

→ Describe the problem. If it's a faulty product, list the date of purchase and the brand and serial or model number. Then say what's wrong with the product. If it's a faulty service, describe the job and name the person who performed it. Give the date and explain what happened.

→ Tell what you've done so far to solve the problem and what solution you'll accept.

"Lemon Laws"

Many states have special laws to protect consumers who buy "lemons." A "lemon" is a new car that keeps breaking down, even after lots of repairs. In some states, a new car is labeled a "lemon" if it spends 30 days or more in the repair shop during its first year. Also, for a car to be a "lemon," the problem has to involve a major part of the car, like the engine or brakes.

To know your rights, look up your state's "lemon law." Also write a letter of complaint to the dealership where you bought the car. Keep records of all the repairs that are made. Also keep copies of your letters and take notes during conversations about the repairs. Generally, the dealer gets to decide whether to repair or replace the car.

→ Give a deadline for a reply—usually, 10 working days. Explain that if you don't have an answer by then, you'll get help from someone else.

6. **Get help.** Several organizations provide help to consumers. Find the phone number of your state's consumer protection agency in the phone book or online. Call the office for advice. Ask to speak with someone who can handle your problem. You can also contact your state's Better Business Bureau (BBB). The BBB collects complaints, answers consumer questions, and helps solve buyer/seller disputes.

Better Business Bureau

The Better Business Bureau (BBB) operates in the United States and Canada. Different BBB offices serve different states, provinces, and regions. To locate the BBB that serves you, look in the phone book or go online (www.bbb.org/us).

You can contact the BBB for either of these reasons:

- **To check on a business:** The BBB reviews businesses and takes complaints from consumers. Contact the BBB to learn about the reputation of a specific business. This is a smart thing to do before hiring a professional service.

- **To file a complaint:** The BBB helps consumers solve problems with products or services they've purchased. The BBB also gets involved in cases of unfair or misleading advertising.

Chapter **3**

Warranties

Always look for a warranty before you buy something expensive. Doing so is especially important if you're buying something mechanical, like a TV or a computer.

Think of a warranty as a promise. It's a promise made to you by the manufacturer or the seller. It guarantees your satisfaction and shows that the manufacturer or seller will stand behind the product.

Read the Warranty

Read the warranty carefully. Most warranties provide this information:

→ **What the manufacturer or seller will do:** The product might be replaced, or it might be repaired. You may or may not have to pay for the repairs, depending on the warranty.

→ **Where to go for repairs:** Many manufacturers have their own repair shops. You may be required to have the repairs done there.

→ **What time period is covered:** Many warranties are good for 90 days after you purchase the product. After that, the manufacturer or seller doesn't have to replace or repair it.

Pay attention to warranties when you *comparison shop.* Getting a good warranty might be worth paying a little more, especially for a major purchase.

Kinds of Warranties

→ **Limited warranties:** Most warranties are limited in two ways. First, they cover only certain kinds of repairs. Usually, repairs are covered when a product breaks down but not when you damage it. The second way most warranties are limited is in terms of time. As mentioned

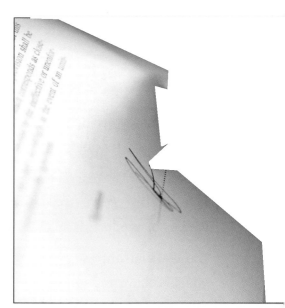

Comparison shop

To look at the same product or service at several different places. The goal is to find the best price or other terms before making a purchase.

earlier, many warranties are limited to 90 days. Others are good for a year or more, but only a few guarantee a product for a lifetime.

→ **Express warranties:** An express warranty is a stated guarantee, either written or oral (spoken). The written warranty that comes with many products is an express warranty.

→ **Implied warranties:** If you don't have an express warranty for a product, there's an *implied* warranty that you'll be satisfied

> **Implied**
> Suggested or understood.

with it. The implied warranty is the law. It protects your right as a consumer to expect high-quality goods. So, even if you don't have a written warranty, you can still make a complaint if something goes wrong.

→ **Extended warranties:** An extended warranty lengthens the period of the original warranty. Usually, you have to buy an extended warranty. It makes sense to buy an extended warranty for an expensive product that's difficult to fix, like a computer. But you probably don't need to buy an extended warranty for an inexpensive product. It could be a waste of money. If you've shopped well and bought a good-quality product, you shouldn't need to repair it for many years to come.

Appliance Warranties

When you buy a new appliance, such as a refrigerator, it's covered by the manufacturer's warranty. That warranty is probably good for 90 days.

If you want a longer period of coverage, you can buy an extended warranty. That warranty will be provided by the store you're buying the appliance from. It will probably cost around $100 and be good for two or three years.

During that time, the warranty will likely cover the costs of parts and labor for making repairs. It may also cover maintenance checks and normal wear-and-tear.

Your Obligations

Again, read every warranty carefully. Make sure you know what your *obligations* are. If you fail to follow certain rules, you could *void* the warranty:

→ The manufacturer may require you to use only authorized repair shops. If you go to an unauthorized shop or try to fix the item yourself, you'll void the warranty.

→ The warranty might require you to show your receipt before having repairs done. Having the receipt proves when you bought the item. It's important in figuring out whether the warranty is still in effect. If you don't have the receipt, you won't be protected by the warranty.

→ The warranty might include requirements for taking care of the product. For instance, a car warranty might require you to have the oil changed every two months. If a problem results from your lack of care, the warranty will be voided.

Obligation

A responsibility or commitment.

Void

To cancel or make worthless.

Tips for Buying an Extended Car Warranty

1. Look at what services are provided, not just the price of the warranty. Try to get a warranty that covers both breakdowns and regular wear-and-tear.

2. Shop around. Talk to the dealership where you bought the car. Also look online for companies that sell extended warranties.

3. Check out the company that's providing the warranty. Contact the Better Business Bureau to learn the company's history and reputation.

4. Look for a warranty that's *transferable*. That means it continues to cover the car after the car has been sold to someone else.

5. If possible, get approval to bring your car into any repair shop. Also try to get towing service covered.

6. Try to avoid having a *deductible*, which means you have to pay a certain cost of the repairs.

Chapter **4**

Telemarketing, Internet, and Trial Offers

Some of the methods used by *telemarketing* and Internet *marketing* are *legitimate.* But not all of them are honest or even legal.

Avoid Scams

Millions of people a year are tricked into buying things by telephone and Internet *scams.* Be cautious when strangers try to sell you something over the phone or using e-mail. In particular, look out for people who do any of the following:

- → Try to pressure or rush you into buying something.

- → Say you've won a prize but ask you to pay for shipping to receive it.

- → Ask you to pay for something in advance.

- → Claim to be someone you know and ask for money to get out of trouble.

- → Ask for personal information, such as your Social Security, bank account, or driver's license number.

- → Tell you to call a long-distance number to enter your name in a sweepstakes.

- → Refuse to give you their names and phone numbers.

Telemarketing

The selling of products and services over the telephone.

Marketing

The business of advertising and selling products and services.

Legitimate

According to rules, standards, or laws.

Scam

A trick or plan that's dishonest and often illegal.

Protect Yourself

→ **Stop the calls:** You don't have to listen to telemarketers. You can ask them to stop calling. Your local phone company or consumer protection agency can tell you how to take action to stop calls, if they continue.

→ **Stop the e-mails:** You don't have to open every e-mail message you receive, either. It's probably best not to open e-mails from people you don't know. Many computers have programs that prevent the delivery of unwanted messages.

→ **Turn down trial offers:** Some companies use "free trial offers" to sell magazines, books, musical recordings, and other items. The companies may even claim that you have "no risk or obligation." But find out for sure. By accepting a trial offer, you may be agreeing to purchase products or services in the future. After the trial

period runs out, you may get billed for a monthly subscription. If you accept a trial offer, cancel the agreement after you've received the free products. Otherwise, you might get billed for additional items, plus shipping and other fees.

Sign Up on the "Do Not Call" List

A law was passed in 2007 that gives Americans the right to stop calls from telemarketers. You can stop getting these calls by signing up on the Do Not Call Registry. You can do this online (www.donotcall.gov) or by phone (1-888-382-1222). Once you sign up, the calls should stop within 31 days. Telemarketers that continue to call can be fined by the US government.

Your phone number is what's listed on the registry, not your name. So, register your cell phone or land-line number to have unwanted calls stopped. (Businesses cannot register.) Your phone number will stay listed unless you call to have it removed (1-888-382-1222).

How to Stop Getting Unwanted E-Mail

The easiest way to stop getting unwanted e-mail is to set up your computer to block or delete these messages. Look for settings that control "junk mail" or "spam." These settings are sometimes called "E-Mail Rules."

You can also stop getting e-mail from specific companies. To do that, open one of these e-mails and go down to the bottom of the message. Look for a link that lets you "unsubscribe." Click on it. Then enter your e-mail address and click the "unsubscribe" button.

Smart Consumer Do's and Don'ts

→ Don't do business with a company that uses only a P.O. box for an address. (If you have a complaint, you may have trouble finding this kind of company.)

→ Do compare the prices at regular stores with the prices in mail, online, or telephone offers. Also keep in mind that by buying at a regular store, you don't have to pay for shipping.

→ Don't give out personal information just because someone asks you for it. Refusing to answer personal questions isn't being rude!

→ Do use common sense. Things that sound too good to be true usually are.

→ Don't send money or give someone your credit card or bank account number to get a free prize, product, or service.

→ Do take the time to understand every offer and talk it over with someone you trust.

Kinds of E-mail Scams

- **Phishing** is a type of scam that asks people to provide personal information. Examples include the numbers and passwords to bank accounts or credit cards.

- A **money-handling scam** uses an innocent person to receive money obtained from an earlier scam. For a small reward, that person puts the money in another account before the scammer moves it elsewhere, usually overseas.

- A **lottery scam** tells someone he or she has won a large amount of money. But to get the money, the person must pay a small fee or provide the numbers to get into his or her bank account.

You Win!

Word List

ability
activity
advertisement
agency
agreement
annual
appliance
approval
arrangements
assembling
attorney
attract
auction
automatic

balance
bargain
beneficiary
branch
brand
budget
bundled

cable
calculate
cancel
carton
catalog
caution
cautious
charges
charity
chemical
chores
claims
classic
classified

co-worker
commit
commitment
communicate
comparison
complaint
conditions
consumer
contact
contribute
convenient
convince
coverage
credit
criminal
customer

damage
data
deadline
defective
delay
delete
delivery
demand
dependent
deposit
description
designed
details
determine
device
disabled
disadvantages
disaster
discount
dispute

donate
dry-clean

e-mail
earnings
embarrassed
emergency
emotional
enforce
entitled
equipment
especially
estimate
exaggerate
exception
exchange
expensive
experienced
expiration
explanation
explore
extended

factor
failure
fee
financially
fined
formal
fraud
furnish
future

garment
goods
guarantee
guidelines

hardware
household

identity
ignore
implied
improper
improve
informal
information
innocent
inspect
install
insurance
interest
interpret
interview
introduce
irregular
issue
item

judgment

key

lapse
legally
legitimate
lender
liable
license
lifestyle
login

maintenance
manager

Word List

marketing
materials
mechanical
membership
mention
merchandise
minimum
misleading

neutral

obligation
obtain
online
option
organized
outlet

package
particular
password
perform
period
permanent
permission
policy
polite
premiums
pressure
principle

priority
privacy
probably
product
professional
program
promptly
protect

qualifications
quality
quantity

rarely
rating
reasoning
receipt
recommend
references
referral
reflect
refund
register
related
relative
rely
remedy
renew
repair
replace

represent
reputation
request
resolve
retail
retire
review
risk
rural

satisfaction
savings
scam
schedule
scheme
seasonal
security
select
shipping
signature
similar
situation
software
solution
specialty
specific
statement
strict
subscription
suitable

support
suspicious

target
telemarketing
terrific
thrift
traffic
transmit
trial

unacceptable
uncomfortable
unfamiliar
unfortunately
unsatisfactory
upcoming

values
vary
ventilation
victim
void

wardrobe
warranty
Wi-Fi
worthwhile

Index

Index

Index